hindu soul

recipes

© Roli & Janssen BV 2007
Published in India by
Roli Books in arrangement with Roli & Janssen
M-75 Greater Kailash II (Market), New Delhi 110 048, India
Ph: ++91-11-29212271, 29212782, 29210886; Fax: (011) 29217185
E-mail: roli@vsnl.com, Website: rolibooks.com

ISBN 978-81-7436-412-8

Editor: Neeta Datta
Design: Arati Subramanyam
Layout: Naresh Mondal and Narendra Shahi
Production: Naresh Nigam and Kumar Raman

Printed and bound in Singapore

TEXT: PUSHPESH PANT

PHOTOGRAPHS: DHEERAJ PAUL

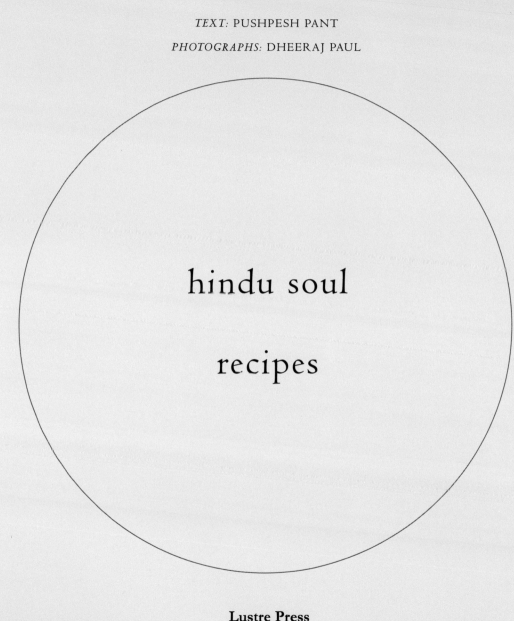

hindu soul

recipes

Lustre Press
Roli Books

To the fond memory of my father,
Dr Krishna Chandra Pant, *rasika* in youth and *virakta* in old age
who taught me through his life the value of *ten tyakten bhujheetha*
(enjoy with a sense of detachment).

Contents

Recipes for Life

HINDU SAGES WHO HAVE EXPOUNDED their philosophy in the *Upanishads* make no distinction between the *atman* (the individual soul) and the *brahman* (the supreme cosmic reality). It is clearly stated *tat tvam asi* (thou art that)! Interestingly an even more ancient Vedic mantra states that *annam vai brahma, annam vai rasah* (*anna* translated as cereals and food is *brahma*). It is *anna* that is the sap or essence of existence. In other words, Hindu soul recipes are recipes for life.

Divinity of food was well recognized in ancient India and the act of imbibing and digesting food was treated akin to performing an *agnihom* (a fire sacrifice). Indeed, imbibing food is like performing the daily *agnihotra* and we can understand why this fascinated our ancestors. Digestion converts matter into energy and this miraculous transformation dramatically unveils the essential unity of matter and energy. Food for the body is unveiled as nourishment for the soul. Confusing dualities can no longer impede us on our journey to liberation from worldly bondage.

Food, especially prepared and partaken, is an integral part of various rites of passage throughout an individual's life. A few months after the birth of a child the ceremony of *annaprashan* is performed when the infant is given the first taste of cooked food weaning him away from mother's milk. The food keeps company of the departed soul even after physical death. Another Upanishadic verse tells us evocatively: *nacha vittein tarpaniyo manushyah* (material riches cannot ensure the deliverance of the soul). It is only the *pinda* (a lump of food) that liberates the soul demolishing *maya* (the illusory web) woven by ignorance that separates the *atma* from the *brahma*.

In *Maitri Upanishad* there are some beautiful lines that illuminate the theme of food: food is verily the highest form of self, truly this life consists of food. If one does not eat his life ebbs, he becomes a non thinker, non seer, non hearer, non speaker and finally, as the vital breath departs, non existent. Food truly…is the source of this world, and the time of food is the time of the sun, the source of time. Let all men, therefore, revere food.

Traditional knowledge preserved in the texts of ayurveda has elaborated on this philosophic basis. Modern medicinal researches have validated many of ayurveda's claims. Many of the ingredients of Hindu soul recipes have proven to have therapeutic value. But, it needs to be reiterated that the beauty of ayurveda is to blend harmoniously the therapeutic with the aesthetic.

Foods, like men, are classified into three types—*satvik*, *rajasik*, and *tamasik* translated as essential/subtle; resplendent/heroic, and gross/inert. Srimad Bhagvad Gita—more commonly known as the Gita—the 'Song Celestial' that encapsulates Sri Krishna's exhortations to the Pandava prince Arjuna, the hero of the Hindu epic Mahabharata on the mythological battlefield of Kurukshetra, has an entire canto devoted to the ayurvedic dietary precepts and correlates these with corresponding personality types.

Swabhava—natural inclination, personal temperament and taste; and *prakriti*—the nature without time and place, the cycle of seasons—are the key concepts that relate food to specific body types and psychological temperament and also establish a correspondence between Man and Nature. *Guna*—inherent properties of ingredients of food—aggravate or sooth the basic humors in our body—*kapha*, *pitta*, and *vata* corresponding to phlegm, bile, and wind. Six basic flavours—*shadrasa* or tastes have specific properties and influence the *guna-dosha*. These are *madhur* (sweet), *amla* (sour), *katu* (bitter), *tikshna* (pungent), *kashaya* (astringent), and *lavana* (salty). Each of these flavours is essential for good health and dining pleasure. The six basic flavours are often compared with the seven basic notes of music and seven hues in the spectrum of colours that may be combined in myriad imaginative ways to create a symphony for the senses.

The cycle of seasons has a remarkable impact on the *kapha-pitta-vata* balance. The classic Sanskrit poem by Kalidasa, the *Ritusamhara* evokes the appropriate mood for a particular season with references to ripening crops and to delicacies associated with specific *barahmasa* (months). The *barahmasa* series of songs mirrors this practice, as do the miniature paintings of the Rajput and Pahari *kalam* (schools). Interestingly, these testify to the percolation of ayurvedic wisdom to the grassroots. In summer, light foods, coolants, and rehydrants are preferred and are on display; in winters, we encounter richer and tonic ingredients that soup up the metabolism.

The dietary wisdom of ayurveda manifests even greater refinement. Systematic observation over generations resulted in accumulation of valuable scientific knowledge. *Vaidyas* (the traditional physicians) learnt from experience that inherent properties of items of food changed with seasons and due to the treatment they received (cooking processes for instance or combining with complimentary or competing ingredients). Ayurvedic lore makes a clear distinction between the 'taste' that our palate discerns and the 'taste' that our body feels after food is digested. *Guna, swada, vipaka, virya* and *prabhava* are five categories through which the metabolic effect of what we eat is finally registered.

Therapeutic is just one dimension of ayurvedic cuisine. No less significant is the aesthetic aspect. Never does ayurveda leave sight of the overarching umbrella of *rasa*—essence of any substance—epitomizing the 'sap of life'. *Rasa* by extension is what is essential to any sensual delight—music and dance, painting and sculpture, and literature all derive their emotive charge from invoking a particular mindset—a mood engendered by permanent and transient emotions. This is the seminal contribution made by the ancient sage Bharat in his famous treatise *Natyashatra*. It is not difficult to appreciate how food is the ultimate mood manipulator. It may be bare nutrition, tonic or intoxicant even toxic at times. It can tranquilize or excite. Ignorance is certainly not bliss in this context.

Of course, ayurveda has many recipes for 'Foods of Ecstacy' (aphrodisiacs, restoratives, tonics). The story of Chyavan rishi, who invented *chyavanprash* to enjoy conjugal bliss in ripe old age, is well-known. But, these are not all.

One of the most famous teachings of the *Upanishads*—compilations of sublime metaphysical speculation in ancient India—is *atmanam viddhi* (Know Thyself): one who intends to embark on the ayurvedic dietary course should follow this precept literally. One must look into the mirror with detachment and candour. Ask the question: Who am I? What is my *swabhav* and *prakriti*? Am I aware of the time and place that I live in? Am I suggestive to the balance or imbalance of *kapha-pitta-vata* in my body? Do I know how the food I imbibe is going to influence my body and mind? Only after these questions have been answered honestly can one begin. The idea is to invite the readers to compose a culinary symphony comprising different harmonious notes to enhance the sensual delight while dining.

Opening one's mind to Hindu soul recipes is to embark on an ecstatic odyssey. Preparing soul-stirring meals each day akin to a culinary symphony resonating harmonious notes ensures that you enjoy continuing good health and celebrate the miracle of life.

Seasons and Food

THE HINDU CALENDAR DIVIDES THE YEAR into six seasons. While in the West, spring, summer, autumn and winter mark easily identifiable quarters, on the Indian subcontinent the rainy season and a sub segment of autumn are allotted an independent seasonal status. This need not confuse those who dwell elsewhere. The wisdom of the ancients incorporated in the soul recipes can be utilized keeping in mind the underlying basic philosophy.

According to ayurveda, seasons are classified into two categories: there are some months in a year that seem to drain or sap our energy. These are called *grahan* (taking away literally). Then there are times when nature appears to be generous with her gifts: we feel full of vim and vigour. Seasons that comprise this segment in the Hindu calendar are aptly called *daan* (gift). Broadly speaking, late spring summer and the rains are *grahan* while autumn and winter are *daan*.

Phalgun and *chaitra* that mark *vasanta* (the spring) in the Indian almanac cover the period from mid-February to mid-April. *Grishma* or summer proper is spread over the next two months and *baisakh* and *jyeshtha* spanning mid-April to mid-June. In fact, the end of spring merges

imperceptibly into summer and often the summer is terminated abruptly by the sudden onset of monsoon. This quartet, according to ayurveda, needs a diet very different from the winter regimen. Cooling and cleansing ingredients are incorporated in traditional recipes; the accent is on bitter and steaming or boiling are preferred to frying.

The three *doshas*—*kapha*, *vata* and *pitta*—are correlated with the elements water, air and fire. One of these elements predominates in a season setting the keynote for it in a manner of speaking. Summer is literally 'fiery' and the rains flood the subcontinent with

water. Both during the summer and the monsoon strong winds are encountered. Quite simply, *pitta* tends to be aggravated in summers and when it rains. It would be wise, therefore, to keep on guard against *vata* too as it can very easily complicate *pitta* and *kapha*

imbalances by stoking the fire and churning the waters. Ingredients that subdue-counteract *pitta-vata* in summer and *kapha-vata* during rains are prescribed in ayurveda to keep one's repose. With the advent of autumn things change. *Pitta* now manifests as a benign influence—the flame that melts the freezing *kapha* blocking the channels in our body. Foods that accelerate the metabolism are considered

tonic in ayurveda. In the lean winter months our body stores fat to use in months ahead and a calorie-rich repast is no longer frowned upon. It is quite remarkable how the two major Hindu festivals, Holi and Diwali, remind us through ritual celebratory menus that it is time to implement seasonal changes in the menu. Obviously, this dietary regimen is not to be followed blindly but applied after appropriate adjustments keeping in mind the individual's body constitution and psychological type. Good health can only be enjoyed when the three *doshas* are in balance—not aggravated by eating against one's grain and oblivious of seasonal imperative.

Soul and the Cosmos

THERE ARE SIX TYPES OF BODY CONSTITUTION: *kapha*, *pitta*, *vata*—the pure types followed by the blends—*kapha-vata*, *kapha-pitta* and *vata-pitta*. In the blends one of the *doshas* may dominate and display its characteristics.

Similarly, there are three pure and two blended temperaments, natural inclinations or psychological orientations: *satvik*, *rajasik*, *tamasik* and *satvik-rajasik*, *rajasik-tamasik*. It is difficult to imagine the coexistence of *satvik* and *tamasik*. The *satvik* type finds it easy to remain tranquil while the *rajasik* is usually restless / agitated. *Tamasik* types are usually phlegmatic. It needs to be added emphatically that this terminology does not imply any superiority or inferiority per se. Most important thing is to know oneself and identify one's nutritional requirements. Remember, what we consume does not only nourish the body but also has a crucial impact on our mind. Food mediates our thoughts and emotions. Interestingly, eating against our natural grain in this context may redress a harmful tendency. This is what soul foods aspire to do.

Snacks

---

raditionally, food in India is not served sequentially (course wise) and 'starters' do not have a separate existence. However, due significance is attached to *uddipaka* (aperitif)—hot or cold—that encourage the digestive gastric juices to flow. These tasty morsels are placed on the plate along with the other items and the diner can according to his preference begin the meal with these or treat them as accompaniments providing a delightful complement or contrast in terms of colour, texture and taste with the main course dishes. These are prepared in accordance with ayurvedic precepts pertaining to *desh-kaal* (time-place) as well as *guna-dosha* (inherent properties of food) to maintain a harmonious relationship between *swabhava* (personality tyle) and *prakriti* (nature-milieu).

Badak

THESE *deep-fried fritters made with black gram paste date back to the Vedic period. These are cooked as ritual offering at festive feasts and also to enrich the everyday menu when a special guest drops in.*

INGREDIENTS

SERVES 4

Split black gram (*urad dal*), soaked for 6 hours
~ ¼ cup / 50 gm / 1¾ oz

Green coriander (*hara dhaniya*), chopped
~ 2 tbsp / 8 gm

Cumin (*jeera*) seeds
~ 1 tbsp / 6 gm

Salt to taste

Green chillies, chopped
~ 3-4

Vegetable oil for deep-frying

METHOD

~ Drain the split black gram and grind till very smooth. Make a thick batter with a little water. Add the green coriander, cumin seeds, salt, and green chillies; mix well.

~ Divide the batter into equal portions. Wet your palm, take a portion and make a patty with a whole in the centre. Make similar patties till all the portions are used up.

~ Heat the oil in a pan; release the patties gently into the oil and deep-fry till golden brown and crisp. Remove with a slotted spoon, and drain the excess oil on absorbent kitchen towels.

~ Serve hot.

Naivedya

Food offered to the deity is *naivedya* derived from *nivedan* (translated as submission). The act it is believed consecrates the offerings and transforms them into *prasad* (graceful blessings). Custom prescribes a specific list of what may be offered to different deities keeping in mind their preferences (and temperament!). Usually *naivedya* comprises items that are purest of the pure—honey, fruits (fresh as well as dried), milk and its derivatives and delicacies prepared with cereals and deep-fried in ghee.

Polika

POPULARLY *called* puri—*completely-puffed up it may be but it is not without reason. This deep-fried bread is prescribed for all ritual celebrations and is considered purest of all.*

INGREDIENTS

MAKES 10

Refined flour (*maida*)
~ **1¾ cups / 250 gm / 9 oz**

For the stuffing:
Black gram (*dhuli urad*), husked, soaked overnight
~ **1⅛ cups / 125 gm / 4 oz**

Aniseed (*saunf*)
~ **1½ tsp / 3¾ gm**

Red chilli powder
~ **½ tsp / 1½ gm**

Ginger (*adrak*), fresh, finely chopped
~ **2 tsp**

Coriander (*dhaniya*) seeds, crushed
~ **3 tsp / 6 gm**

Green coriander (*hara dhaniya*), fresh, finely chopped
~ **2 tsp**

Vegetable oil / Ghee for deep-frying

METHOD

~ **For the stuffing,** drain the soaked black gram and grind to a smooth and stiff paste. Mix in the remaining ingredients.

~ Take the flour and heap it in a mound on a flat surface. Make a hollow in the centre and pour a little water, mix well and knead to obtain slightly hard dough.

~ Divide the dough into 10 equal portions and shape into small balls. Flatten between moist palms.

~ Put 1 level tsp of the stuffing in the centre and bring the edges together to enclose the filling completely. Reshape into balls, flatten and roll out carefully into discs.

~ Heat the oil / ghee in a *kadhai* (wok); deep-fry the discs till they puff up and acquire a golden hue. Remove and drain the excess oil absorbent kitchen towels.

Purnima

PURNIMA—*the night of full moon—is what this* satvik *dish with a thousand-year-old ancestry immediately brings to mind. It is commonly known as* idli.

METHOD

~ Soak the black gram and rice in water overnight.

~ Drain and grind with semolina to fine and smooth paste. Add baking powder and salt, whip briskly for a minute.

~ Spoon out the batter into moulds or small bowls lined with cloth, and steam for about 10 minutes. Remove the rice cakes and serve hot.

INGREDIENTS

SERVES 4-5

Black gram (*dhuli urad*), husked
~ **½ cup / 100 gm / 3½ oz**

Rice, parboiled
~ **¾ cup / 150 gm / 5 oz**

Semolina (*suji*)
~ **¾ cup / 150 gm / 5 oz**

Baking powder
~ **1 tsp / 6 gm**

Salt to taste

Trishna Nigrahan

Literally, insatiable thirst, it is also a metaphor for desire that never ceases. Ayurveda categorizes thirst according to local or systemic causes. Parched throat or mouth are symptoms of local thirst while dehydration debilitates body due to systemic causes. If thirst is not quenched the mind is restless and the soul disturbed. Ingredients like lemon, oranges, pomegranate, cardamom, and grapes are reckoned as *trishna nigrahan* (thirst retardants).

Purika

MORE *a substantial snack than a staff of life.* Purika, *the spicy, stuffed version of* polika, *is commonly known as* kachori.

INGREDIENTS

MAKES 12

Refined flour (*maida*)
~ 3½ cups / 500 gm / 1.1 lb

Salt
~ a pinch

Baking powder
~ 1 tsp / 6 gm

Ghee
~ 4 tbsp / 60 gm / 2 oz

For the stuffing:
Split black gram (*urad dal*), soaked for 45 minutes
~ ⅓ cup / 65 gm / 2¼ oz

Vegetable oil
~ 2 tbsp / 30 ml / 1 fl oz

Ginger (*adrak*), chopped
~ 2 tbsp / 15 gm

Green chillies, chopped
~ 1 tbsp / 6 gm

Red chilli powder
~ 2 tsp / 6 gm

Fennel (*moti saunf*) powder
~ 1½ tsp / 4½ gm

Cumin (*jeera*) powder
~ 1½ tsp / 4½ gm

Asafoetida (*hing*)
~ a pinch

Coriander (*dhaniya*) powder
~ 1 tsp / 3 gm

Sugar
~ ½ tsp

Salt to taste

Vegetable oil for deep-frying

METHOD

~ Sieve the flour with salt and baking powder. Add the ghee and rub between your fingers to get breadcrumb texture. Pour water, mix and knead to obtain soft dough. Cover with a moist cloth and keep aside.

~ **For the stuffing**, drain and coarsely grind the split black gram with little water.

~ Heat the oil in a pan; add ginger, green chillies, and the remaining ingredients except sugar and salt. Stir well. Add ground dal and cook till all the moisture is dried. Add sugar and salt; mix well. Remove and keep aside to cool.

~ Divide the dough into 12 equal portions and shape into balls. Flatten the balls slightly with your palm. Place a little stuffing in the centre and bring the edges together to form balls, flatten slightly.

~ Heat the oil in a pan; deep-fry in batches on low heat until golden brown and crisp. Remove and drain the excess oil on absorbent kitchen towels.

~ Serve hot.

Dhokla

LIGHT *as air, sweet-n-sour diamonds fashioned out of nutritious gram flour—steamed then spiked with a tempering of green chillies and mustard.*

INGREDIENTS

SERVES 6

Bengal gram (*chana dal*),
soaked overnight
~ 2½ cups / 500 gm / 1.1 lb

Lukewarm water
~ 1 cup / 240 ml / 8 fl oz

Vegetable oil
~ 4 tbsp / 60 ml / 2 fl oz

Ginger (*adrak*), chopped
~ 1" piece

Green chillies, coarsely
grounded
~ a few

Sugar
~ 1 tsp / 3 gm

Soda bicarbonate
~ 1 tsp / 6 gm

Salt to taste

Juice of lemons (*nimbu*)
~ 4

Green chillies, whole, slit
~ 6-7

Black mustard seeds (*rai*)
~ 2 tsp / 6 gm

Curry leaves (*kadhi patta*)
~ 10-15

METHOD

~ Drain and grind the Bengal gram to a soft paste of dropping consistency.

~ In the lukewarm water, add the oil, ginger, green chillies, sugar, soda bicarbonate, salt, and lemon juice. Mix well and add to the above batter.

~ Preheat a steamer and grease the container. Pour in the batter half filling the heated container. Cover and steam for about 5 minutes. Remove and cut into squares immediately.

~ Heat 2 tbsp oil in a pan to smoking; lower heat and add the whole green chillies, black mustard seeds, and curry leaves. When the seeds start to splutter, remove and pour over the steamed squares.

Ikshu

Ayurveda recognized the beneficial properties of *ikshu* (sugarcane) and considered it a tonic, revitalizer, blood purifier, emollient and diuretic. *Sharkara* or sugar is mentioned in the famous *Yogasutra* of sage Patanjali who hailed from the Punjab. Kautilya in his treatise on statecraft, the *Arthashastra*, lists a range of sugar products including *phanit* (molasses) and *khand* (raw sugar crystals). Emperor Harsha in the seventh century AD received an embassy from China that wished to study sugar manufacturing. None can dispute that the Indians were the first to taste sugar and share it with the rest of the world.

Anupama

LITERALLY *quite incomparable is (called* upama *in South India) a popular breakfast item or a late afternoon snack. Requiring just a hint of fat to cook, wholemeal semolina has enough fiber to keep the health-conscious happy.*

INGREDIENTS

SERVES 4

Semolina (*suji*), coarse
~ 1 cup / 200 gm / 7 oz

Vegetable oil / Ghee
~ ½ cup / 120 ml / 4 fl oz

Ginger (*adrak*), ground
~ 1 tsp / 6 gm

Bengal gram (*chana dal*)
~ 1 tsp

Black gram (*dhuli urad*), husked
~ 1 tsp

Mustard seeds (*rai*)
~ ½ tsp / 1½ gm

Cumin (*jeera*) seeds
~ ½ tsp / 1 gm

Cashew nuts (*kaju*)
~ 6-8

Green chillies, chopped
~ 4

Salt to taste

Green coriander (*hara dhaniya*), chopped
~ 1 bunch

Juice of lemon (*nimbu*)
~ 1

METHOD

~ Heat half the oil / ghee in a frying pan; add ginger and stir. Add Bengal gram, black gram, mustard seeds, cumin seeds, and cashew nuts; fry for a while. Add green chillies and cook on low heat for about 3-4 minutes.

~ Meanwhile, heat 2 cups of water separately.

~ Add salt and semolina to the seasoning mixture in the frying pan. Pour in the hot water and stir continuously till all the water is absorbed. Add the remaining oil / ghee and green coriander; mix and remove from heat.

~ Add lemon juice and serve hot.

Ardrak

The Chinese travellers, I Ching and Xuan Zang, have mentioned the use of ginger as a flavouring agent in the dining halls of the Buddhist monasteries they visited. Ginger is used both green and in dried form and has a pleasantly astringent taste. It is also valued as an aperitif and digestive. Dried ginger has pronounced pungency. Ginger, growing underground is eschewed by orthodox Jains but even strict vegetarian Hindus consider it *satvik*.

Dosai

A *pancake-like bread, the* dosai *is the inseparable companion of many main-course dishes in South India. Encountered in many avatars—either crisp and paper thin or spongy and plump—it is an exceptional one-dish meal.*

METHOD

~ Drain and grind the rice to a thick, grainy paste.

~ Drain and grind the black gram with fenugreek seeds to fine paste.

~ Mix the rice paste and black gram paste together and let this mixture stand overnight. Add salt to taste.

~ Heat a large non-stick frying pan or a large, flat *tawa* (griddle); pour a ladle of the batter in the centre. Spread the batter in a circular motion with the back of the spoon to a thin layer. Allow it to cook on medium heat until dry, spread some ghee or oil in the centre and along the sides and cook till the pancake is golden and crisp. Roll it up and remove. Repeat till all the batter is used up.

~ Serve at once with chutney.

INGREDIENTS

SERVES 4

Rice, parboiled, soaked overnight
~ ¾ cup / 150 gm / 5 oz

Black gram (*urad dal*), soaked overnight
~ ¾ cup / 150 gm / 5 oz

Fenugreek seeds (*methi dana*)
~ 1 tsp / 4½ gm

Ghee / Vegetable oil for frying

Salt to taste

Rajarasika

POLIKA *in its most richest and tantalizing incarnation. This deep-fried shell serves as an edible container for assorted savouries to provide a delicious snack that can substitute at a pinch for a light one-dish meal.*

INGREDIENTS

SERVES 6-8

Refined flour (*maida*)
~ **3½ cups / 500 gm / 1.1 lb**

Semolina (*suji*)
~ **¾ cup / 150 gm / 5 oz**

Salt to taste

Baking powder
~ **½ tsp / 3 gm**

Vegetable oil
~ **3 tbsp / 45 ml / 1½ fl oz**

For the filling:
Red chilli powder
~ **1½ tbsp / 13½ gm**

Green chillies, chopped
~ **5**

Chick peas (*kabuli chana*),
boiled
~ **1 cup / 150 gm / 5 oz**

Split green gram (*moong dal*), boiled
~ **¾ cup / 150 gm / 5 oz**

Sprouted beans
~ **125 gm / 4 oz**

Vegetable oil for frying

Tamarind chutney
~ **100 gm / 3½ oz**

Mint chutney
~ **100 gm / 3½ oz**

Yoghurt (*dahi*), whisked
~ **100 gm / 3½ oz**

Green coriander (*hara dhaniya*), chopped
~ **a large sprig**

METHOD

~ Sieve the flour, semolina, salt, and baking powder together. Add warm oil and knead into stiff dough. Leave to rise.

~ **For the filling,** mix all the ingredients together.

~ Divide the dough equally into 15-20 balls. Flatten the balls slightly with your palm. Place a little stuffing in the centre and bring the edges together to form balls, flatten slightly.

~ Roll the balls with a rolling pin into discs of about 4" diameter.

~ Heat the oil in a *kadhai* (wok); deep-fry the discs, turning, till evenly coloured. Remove and drain the excess oil. Keep aside to cool.

~ Make a hole on top of each disc and stuff with the filling mixture. Pour the chutneys and yoghurt. Serve garnished with green coriander and drizzle with sprinkling masala (made by mixing together 1 tsp each of dried pomegranate seeds, powdered sugar, and cumin seeds, ½ tsp each of rock salt, dried mango powder and clove powder).

Khandita

THE *name literally translated as 'broken' implies a heroin jilted by her lover (broken-hearted). Although cut thus broken into bite-size pieces, this savoury roll has never lacked loyal admirers.*

INGREDIENTS

SERVES 4-6

Gram flour (*besan*)
~ **1 cup / 100 gm / 3½ oz**

Yoghurt (*dahi*)
~ **1 cup / 250 gm / 9 oz**

Ginger (*adrak*) paste
~ **1 tsp / 6 gm**

Turmeric (*haldi*) powder
~ **¼ tsp**

Salt to taste

Green chilli paste
~ **1 tsp / 5 gm**

Red chilli powder to taste

For the tempering:
Vegetable oil
~ **1 tbsp / 15 ml**

Fenugreek seeds (*methi dana*)
~ **1 tsp / 4½ gm**

Cumin (*jeera*) seeds
~ **1 tsp / 2 gm**

Asafoetida (*hing*)
~ **¼ tsp**

Dried red chillies (*sookhi lal mirch*)
~ **2**

Sesame (*til*) seeds
~ **1 tsp / 3 gm**

Curry leaves (*kadhi patta*)
~ **1 tbsp**

METHOD

~ Make a smooth paste with gram flour, yoghurt, ginger paste, turmeric powder, water, and salt.

~ Pour this mixture in a *kadhai* (wok) and cook till thick. Grease a flat tray and spread this mixture thinly over it.

~ When it sets, roll from one end to another, like a swiss roll. Cut into 3 cm pieces and keep aside.

~ **For the tempering**, heat the oil and add all the ingredients. Cook for a few minutes then pour this over the little pieces and serve.

Til

The sesame seed is called *til* in Sanskrit and is the word from which *taila*, the generic term for oil, is derived. It continues to be a popular cooking medium both in North and South India. The sesame seeds, both white and black, are used in religious rituals and are valued for their nutty taste, subtle aroma, and nutritional properties. Coupled with jaggery they are used to make delicious confections in the countryside during the winter months. *Til* is used in a variety of ways. It is cooked with rice and vegetables and relished roasted or pounded.

Main Course

The staples in India are unleavened bread made with wheat, millet, barley or maize flour in the north and west, and steamed rice in the south and east. These are paired with lentils, legumes, and seasonal vegetables to ensure that the body gets a balanced nutritious meal. As a matter of fact, dal-roti or dal-*chawal* (rice) or their equivalent in different regional languages are synonymous with basic sustenance.

Easily digestible vegetable proteins are provided by lentils and the essentially vegetarian 'accompaniments' to bread or rice take care of the daily requirements of vitamins and minerals. Home recipes in most parts of the country rely on minimal cooking of leafy vegetables—stir-frying and steaming. Deep-frying is usually reserved for special festive feasts.

Shyama

SHYAMA *or black in this case is not only beautiful but bountiful also. Cooked traditionally in a cast-iron vessel, this lentil soup is rich in easily digestible proteins and laced with traces of minerals.*

INGREDIENTS

SERVES 4-6

Soya beans (black)
~ **½ cup / 100 gm / 3½ oz**

French beans (*rajmah chitral*)
~ **½ cup / 100 gm / 3½ oz**

Kidney beans (*rajmah*)
~ **½ cup / 100 gm / 3½ oz**

Black gram (*dhuli urad*), unhusked
~ **½ cup / 100 gm / 3½ oz**

Bengal gram (*chana dal*), unhusked
~ **½ cup / 100 gm / 3½ oz**

Pigeon peas (*lobiya*)
~ **¼ cup / 50 gm / 1¾ oz**

Coriander (*dhaniya*) powder
~ **2 tbsp / 18 gm**

Cumin (*jeera*) powder
~ **2 tbsp / 18 gm**

Salt to taste

For the tempering:
Ghee
~ **1 tbsp / 15 gm**

Jambu (Himalayan chives if not available use 2 whole red chillies paired with 4-5 cloves of garlic)
~ **a generous pinch**

For the garnishing:
Green coriander (*hara dhaniya*), chopped
~ **a large sprig**

METHOD

~ Clean and wash the lentils well and soak overnight in water. Drain and cook in a pressure cooker with enough water to cover for about 30 minutes. Keep aside to cool before opening to release the pressure. Mash the mixture a little with a spatula employing a gentle touch.

~ Transfer the mixture to a caste-iron wok (*kadhai*). Add the water in which the lentils have been cooked along with coriander powder, cumin powder, and salt; cook on low medium heat for about 2 hours. Remove the lentil grains from the soup. Ideally, the mixture should have a thick consistency and a creamy texture.

~ **For the tempering**, heat the ghee, add the *jambu* or garlic cloves and whole red chillies. When the *jambu* releases its aroma or the garlic cloves turn dark brown or the chillies begin to change colour, pour over the mixture.

~ Serve hot garnished with green coriander and accompanied with steamed rice.

Rajmasha

THE *king of all* masha *(lentils), is the name given to red kidney beans that in popular parlance has become* rajmah. *This important source of protein in the vegetarian diet reigns supreme in the Vale of Kashmir.*

INGREDIENTS

SERVES 4-6

Red kidney beans
(*rajmah*), soaked overnight
~ 2½ cups / 500 gm / 1.1 lb

Green cardamom (*choti elaichi*)
~ 8

Black cardamom (*badi elaichi*)
~ 6

Cinnamon (*dalchini*) sticks,
2" each
~ 4

Turmeric (*haldi*) powder
~ 1 tsp / 3 gm

Dried ginger powder
(*sonth*)
~ 1½ tsp / 4½ gm

Salt to taste

Kashmiri red chilli powder,
dissolved in 2 tbsp water
~ 1½ tsp / 4½ gm

Butter
~ 3 tbsp / 45 gm / 1¼ oz

METHOD

~ Drain and boil the red kidney beans in enough water to cover till soft. Retain the water.

~ Put the boiled kidney beans, water, green and black cardamoms, cinnamon sticks, turmeric powder, dried ginger powder, salt, and red chilli water in a pan; bring the mixture to the boil. Cover and cook on low heat until the beans are tender and gravy is quite thick.

~ Add the butter and serve hot with steamed rice.

Upavasa

Hindus firmly believe that fasting is an integral part of nourishing the body and soul. Traditionally people were encouraged to fast on certain days of the week according to their choice; it is not necessary to eschew food entirely, partial renunciation is often enough. *Upavasa* helps us appreciate the significance of self-discipline and balance in life—particularly in the sphere of dietetics.

Pushpanjali

AN *offering of* pushpanjali, *palm full of fragrant flowers, at the feet of the deity or a revered person is the traditional form of homage. The diner is greeted in a like manner by this 'floral tribute'.*

INGREDIENTS

SERVES 5-6

For the koftas:
Raw bananas, boiled, peeled, mashed
~ **500 gm / 1.1 lb**

Green coriander (*hara dhaniya*)
~ **2½ cups / 120 gm / 4 oz**

Green chillies, finely chopped
~ **4-5**

Turmeric (*haldi*) powder
~ **1½ tsp / 4½ gm**

Green chilli paste
~ **3 tbsp / 45 gm / 1½ oz**

Salt to taste

Garam masala
~ **1½ tsp / 4½ gm**

Gram flour (*besan*)
~ **2 tbsp / 20 gm**

For the filling:
Banana flower (*mocha*) boiled, chopped, squeezed dry
~ **1 medium-sized**

Vegetable oil for deep-frying

Coconut (*nariyal*), grated
~ **½ cup / 60 gm / 2 oz**

Ground nuts (*moongphalli*)
~ **¼ cup / 35 gm / 1¼ oz**

Butter
~ **1 tbsp / 15 gm**

Cumin (*jeera*) seeds
~ **1 tsp / 2 gm**

Salt to taste

Coriander (*dhaniya*) powder
~ **1 tbsp / 9 gm**

Yoghurt (*dahi*), hung, whisked
~ **1 cup / 250 gm / 9 oz**

Green peas (*hara mater*), shelled, boiled, mashed
~ **2½ cups / 400 gm / 14 oz**

Sugar
~ **2 tbsp / 30 gm**

Lemon (*nimbu*) juice
~ **1 tsp / 5 ml**

METHOD

~ **For the koftas**, mix all the ingredients together and divide the mixture into equal portions and shape into balls.

~ Flatten the balls and put a little banana flower filling in the middle. Reshape into koftas.

~ Heat the oil in a pan; deep-fry the koftas on low medium heat till rich golden in colour. Remove and drain the excess oil on absorbent kitchen towels. Keep aside.

~ Pan roast the coconut and ground nuts and grind to paste.

~ Melt the butter in a pan; add the cumin seeds. When the seeds start spluttering, add salt, and coriander powder dissolved in 2 tbsp water; stir-fry for about 2 minutes. Add the yoghurt and stir to blend well.

~ Now add the mashed peas with the coconut paste and cook for 3-4 minutes. Add 1 cup water and bring to the boil, reduce heat and simmer. Stir in the sugar. Gently add the koftas in the gravy and simmer for about 2 minutes. Sprinkle the lemon juice and stir gently. Remove and adjust the seasoning.

Mrinalini

LOTUS *symbolizes awakening of spiritual intelligence and liberation. This can only be accomplished when the bonds of attachment are broken. Lotus stems* (mrinal) *have inspired gifted cooks to create delicacies like* mrinalini, *tantalizingly tranquil.*

INGREDIENTS

SERVES 5-6

Lotus stems (*kamal kakri*), cut diagonally into 1½" pieces
~ 1 kg / 2.2 lb

Water
~ 6 cups / 1.5 lt / 48 fl oz

Ghee
~ ⅓ cup / 70 gm / 2¼ oz

Black cardamom (*badi elaichi*)
~ 4

Green cardamom (*choti elaichi*)
~ 8

Cloves (*laung*)
~ 8

Cinnamon (*dalchini*), 1" sticks
~ 4

Yoghurt (*dahi*),hung to remove water
~ 2 cups / 500 gm / 1.1 lb

Aniseed (*saunf*) powder
~ 2 tsp / 6 gm

Dried ginger powder (*sonth*)
~ 2 tsp / 6 gm

Salt to taste

Dried mint (*pudina*) leaves
~ ½ tsp

Black cumin (*shah jeera*) seeds
~ ½ tsp

METHOD

~ Boil the lotus stems in water and cook until half done.

~ Heat the ghee in another pan; add the black and green cardamoms, cloves, and cinnamon sticks. When these change colour reduce heat and slowly add yoghurt stirring constantly to avoid curdling. Add aniseed powder, dried ginger powder, and salt. Stir well and cook for about 10 minutes.

~ Add the half-cooked lotus stems; reduce heat and simmer till tender. Add the dried mint leaves and black cumin seeds. Blend well.

Palankya

THIS *delightfully different spinach dish* (palankya) *is from the Himalayan state of Uttaranchal. Its porridge-like consistency is considered wholesome and nourishing for the soul.*

INGREDIENTS

SERVES 4

Spinach (*palak*), washed, cleaned
~ 1 kg / 2.2 lb

Vegetable oil
~ 1 tbsp / 15 ml

Asafoetida (*hing*)
~ a pinch

Onions, medium-sized, finely sliced, optional
~ 2

Ginger (*adrak*) paste
~ 1 tbsp / 18 gm

Green chillies
~ 3-4

Rice flour
~ 2 tbsp / 20 gm

Salt to taste

Ghee
~ 1 tbsp / 15 gm

Dried red chillies (*sookhi lal mirch*)
~ 2-3

Garlic (*lasan*) cloves, optional
~ 6

Ginger, cut into thin strips
~ 2"

METHOD

~ Boil the spinach in 1 cup of water for a few minutes. Remove and mash with a wooden churner. (The mixie is avoidable). Keep aside.

~ Heat the oil in a thick-bottomed pan; add asafoetida and sauté till it dissolves. Add the onions, stir-fry till translucent. Add ginger paste and continue to stir-fry for about a minute.

~ Add the spinach purée and green chillies. Pour 2 cups of hot water and mix well. Slowly add the rice flour, stirring continuously to ensure no lumps are formed. Bring to the boil. Sprinkle salt and reduce heat to low-medium and cook uncovered for about 20 minutes.

~ Heat the ghee in a pan; add the dried red chillies and garlic cloves (optional). When these change colour, remove and pour over the spinach mixture.

~ Serve hot garnished with ginger strips and accompanied with rice or roti.

Pindalukam

ALU *originally* alukam *in Sanskrit today is synonymous with potato brought to the Indies by the Portuguese. This recipe uses* arvi *that is called* pinalu *in the Himalayan state of Uttaranchal derived from* pindalukam *in Sanskrit.*

METHOD

~ Heat 2 tbsp ghee in a thick-bottomed pan; add cumin seeds. When these begin to crackle, add ginger and garlic. Stir-fry on medium heat for about 30 seconds. Add the onions and continue to fry till onions turn light brown.

~ Add the colocasia and stir-fry for about 5 minutes. Add all the powdered spices and salt; mix well. Pour 1 cup of water and bring to the boil. Reduce heat to low, cover the pan, and cook for about 20 minutes, stirring occasionally to ensure that the mixture does not stick to the bottom.

~ Add yoghurt, stirring constantly with a light touch so as not to mash the vegetable. Cook for another 20 minutes.

~ Heat the remaining ghee in a pan and when smoking hot, add the dried red chillies. When the chillies change colour, pour over the vegetable mixture.

~ Serve hot garnished with green coriander and accompanied with roti or rice.

INGREDIENTS

SERVES 4

Colocasia (*arvi*), peeled, cut into pieces
~ **1 kg / 2.2 lb**

Ghee
~ **3 tbsp / 45 gm / 1½ oz**

Cumin (*jeera*) seeds
~ **1 tsp / 2 gm**

Ginger (*adrak*), thinly sliced
~ **2"**

Garlic (*lasan*) cloves, thinly sliced
~ **8-10**

Onions, medium-sized, thinly sliced
~ **2**

Coriander (*dhaniya*) powder
~ **2 tsp / 6 gm**

Cumin powder
~ **1 tsp / 3 gm**

Red chilli powder
~ **1 tsp / 3 gm**

Turmeric (*haldi*) powder
~ **½ tsp**

Salt to taste

Yoghurt (*dahi*), beaten
~ **200 gm / 7 oz**

Dried red chillies (*sookhi lal mirch*)
~ **2**

Green coriander (*hara dhaniya*), chopped for garnishing
~ **a few sprigs**

Santosham

IT *is well said that* santosham paramam sukham *(contentment with little that is available is bliss); and this simple yet immensely satisfying recipe for knol khol from the Kashmir repertoire seems to illustrate this brilliantly.*

INGREDIENTS

SERVES 4-6

Knol khol (*ganth gobi*)
with leaves
~ **1 kg / 2.2 lb**

Ghee / Vegetable oil
~ **125 gm / 4 oz**

Asafoetida (*hing*)
~ **a pinch**

Cloves (*laung*)
~ **2**

Green chillies
~ **4**

Coriander (*dhaniya*)
powder
~ **1 tsp / 3 gm**

Bari (dried spice tablet
incorporating aromatic
Kashmiri garam masala)
~ **1 tsp**

Dried ginger powder
(*sonth*)
~ **1 tsp / 3 gm**

Salt to taste

METHOD

~ Heat the ghee or oil in a pan; add asafoetida and cloves. When the cloves change colour add the knol khol. Shake the vessel, cover and simmer on low heat for 10 minutes.

~ Add the remaining ingredients and stir-fry for 2-3 minutes. Add 1 cup water and simmer on low heat for about 15 minutes.

~ Serve hot.

Agnihom

Agnihom, literally fire ritual, symbolizes the 'digestive fire'—a manifestation of one of the five *mahabhutas* (the great elements) which represents the flame provided by the ritual altar and food, we are told, should be approached with the same reverence that is accorded to consecrated offerings. According to the rituals, before putting a morsel in the mouth one was duty bound to offer food to *prithvi* (Mother Earth), the guests, and the cow.

Amulya

THIS *is where the usually overlooked Cinderella-like radish becomes a princess quite priceless* (amulya); *its pungency removed or at least rendered mild when paired with ridged gourd.*

INGREDIENTS

SERVES 4

Radish (*mooli*), tender, washed, scraped, cut into 2-3" pieces
~ 500 gm / 1.1 lb

Ridged gourd (*torai*), scraped, washed, cut into round slices ¼" thickness
~ 500 gm / 1.1 lb

Mustard (*sarson*) oil
~ 2 tbsp / 30 ml / 1 fl oz

Cumin (*jeera*) seeds
~ ½ tsp / 1 gm

Coriander (*dhaniya*) powder
~ 1 tsp / 3 gm

Cumin (*jeera*) powder
~ ½ tsp / 1½ gm

Turmeric (*haldi*) powder
~ ¼ tsp

Salt to taste

Green chillies, long
~ 2-3

METHOD

~ Heat the oil to smoking in a thick-bottomed pan; add cumin seeds. When they begin to crackle, add the radish, coriander powder, cumin powder, turmeric powder, and salt; stir well for a couple of minutes.

~ Add the ridged gourd and mix well. Cook, preferably uncovered, on low heat, stirring frequently till the vegetables are cooked but retain a little bite. Add the green chillies and cook for another 45 seconds.

~ Serve hot with roti.

Paan

According to food historians, the betel leaf is an import from the Southeast Asia. Since its arrival in India, more than two millennia ago, it has become an integral part of not only fine dining but also of rituals. Puja begins with it—*patram pushpam phalam toyam* (the barest essentials that may be offered to a deity). It is chewed as an after-meal digestive and a mouth freshener. The leaf is astringent, aromatic and carminative.

Karuvelvilas

BITTER *as beautiful' is the best description of the gourd that according to its Sanskrit name playfully adorns a vine. This vegetable is considered extremely beneficial in ayurveda—a blood purifier and effective in regulating the metabolism of sugar.*

INGREDIENTS

SERVES 4-6

Bitter gourd (*karela*), washed, scraped
~ 12

Salt to taste

Vegetable oil for deep-frying

Cumin (*jeera*) seeds
~ ½ tsp / 1 gm

Ginger (*adrak*) paste
~ 1 tsp / 6 gm

Garlic (*lasan*) paste
~ 1 tsp / 6 gm

Green chillies
~ 2-3

Red chilli powder
~ ¼ tsp

Turmeric (*haldi*) powder
~ ¼ tsp

METHOD

~ Rub the bitter gourd with salt; arrange on a tilting tray and reserve for at least 2 hours. Then slice into thin rounds.

~ Heat the oil in a frying pan; add cumin seeds and stir on medium heat until they begin to pop. Add ginger-garlic paste and green chillies; sauté until the garlic is lightly coloured. Then add the red chilli powder and turmeric powder. Add the bitter gourd and fry till dark brown and crisp.

Charuchanak

GREEN *gram is indeed 'beautiful to behold' as indicated by its name in this refreshing, nourishing incarnation. This snack is more commonly prepared with fresh green peas.*

INGREDIENTS

SERVES 4-6

Green gram (*boot/choliya*)
~ **1 kg / 2.2 lb**

Ghee
~ **2 tbsp / 30 gm / 1 oz**

Asafoetida (*hing*)
~ **a pinch**

Coriander (*dhaniya*)
powder
~ **½ tsp / 1½ gm**

Green chillies, deseeded,
sliced
~ **5**

Salt to taste

Lemon (*nimbu*) juice
~ **2 tbsp / 30 ml / 1 fl oz**

METHOD

~ Remove stems from the green gram and soak in water for a few minutes. Drain the water and keep aside.

~ Heat the ghee in a pan; add and dissolve the asafoetida in it. Add the green gram and stir after sprinkling coriander powder, stir-fry for about a minute. Add green chillies and salt; cook for 7-8 minutes, stirring occasionally and sprinkling very little water to keep the dish moist. Squeeze lemon juice before serving.

Jalam

Life began in water and, according to Hindu myths, ends in water with the epochal grand deluge (the *pralay*). Ancient Indians differentiated between celestial and terrestrial sources of water. Rain and snow fall from the skies and are believed to have celestial origins. Water obtained from the rivers, springs and wells is classed as earthly. The best is believed to be *Gangajal* which is likened with nectar, this is because the river Ganga is believed to have descended from the heavens.

Suparna

THE *Hindus have always been partial to the cabbage called* gojivha *due to its resemblance to a cow's tongue, from which the vernacular* gobi *is derived. We prefer to address this stir-fried South Indian preparation as* suparna *which means a noble leaf.*

INGREDIENTS

SERVES 4

Green cabbage (*bandh gobi*), washed well, finely shredded
~ 250 gm / 9 oz

Vegetable oil
~ 3 tbsp / 45 ml / 1½ fl oz

Mustard seeds (*rai*)
~ 1 tsp / 3 gm

Bengal gram (*chana dal*)
~ 1 tsp

Black gram (*urad dal*)
~ 1 tsp

Curry leaves (*kadhi patta*)
~ 20

Green chillies, fresh, cut into long slivers
~ 2-4

Salt to taste

Coconut (*nariyal*), freshly grated
~ 3 tbsp

METHOD

~ Heat the oil in a large frying pan on medium heat; add the mustard seeds. When the seeds start to splutter, add the Bengal gram and black gram and stir-fry until the dals change colour. Add the curry leaves and stir for a few seconds.

~ Add green chillies and stir again. Add the cabbage. Stir once to mix. Add salt and mix again. Cover, turn heat to low, and cook for 5-6 minutes or until the cabbage is cooked and is nicely glazed but retains its crunch.

~ Remove the cover. Add the coconut and mix well, stirring vigorously for a minute or so.

~ Serve hot.

Kanchanjhangha

THE *stem of the banana tree has inspired poets to use it as a simile for beautifully proportioned thighs resplendent as if cast in gold* (kanchanjhangha). *The poetic license is evoked while naming this delicacy.*

METHOD

~ Remove the outer skin of the stem and cut into slices. Then cut these slices into pieces. Add the green gram, salt, and the buttermilk; mix well. Keep aside for about 15 minutes.

~ Heat the oil in a pan; add mustard seeds. When the seeds start to splutter, add black gram and dried red chilli; stir-fry for a minute.

~ Drain the buttermilk mixture and add the vegetable mix to the pan; keep stirring on low heat. After the vegetable is cooked, add the coconut and mix well. Simmer for 2 more minutes.

~ Remove and serve hot with steamed rice.

INGREDIENTS

SERVES 4

Banana stem
~ **1 foot long**

Green gram (*moong dal*)
~ **2 tsp**

Salt to taste

Buttermilk (*chaas*), sour
~ **1 cup / 200 ml / 7 fl oz**

Vegetable oil
~ **1 tsp / 5 ml**

Mustard seeds (*rai*)
~ **½ tsp / 1½ gm**

Black gram (*urad dal*)
~ **1 tsp**

Dried red chilli (*sookhi lal mirch*)
~ **1**

Coconut (*nariyal*), grated
~ **2 tsp**

Kandananda

WHO *would have thought that yam can be so blissful; it is substantial, nutritious, ready-to-absorb myriad flavours which it readily imparts to the diner. The yam that gives unalloyed joy is what the name translates.*

INGREDIENTS

SERVES 4

Yam (*jimikand*), peeled, washed, cut into 3 cm cubes
~ **500 gm / 1.1 lb**

Banana, unripe, peeled, slit lengthwise, cut into 1 cm cubes
~ **20 gm**

Red chilli powder
~ **1 tsp / 3 gm**

Turmeric (*haldi*) powder
~ **¼ tsp**

Salt
~ **1 tsp / 3 gm**

Ground to a paste:
Coconut (*nariyal*), fresh, medium-sized, grated
~ **½**

Cumin (*jeera*) seeds
~ **½ tsp / 1 gm**

Water
~ **½ cup / 120 ml / 4 fl oz**

For the tempering:
Coconut oil
~ **2 tbsp / 30 ml / 1 fl oz**

Mustard seeds (*rai*)
~ **2 tsp / 6 gm**

Dried red chillies (*sookhi lal mirch*), torn into pieces
~ **3**

Coconut, fresh, medium-sized, grated
~ **½**

Curry leaves (*kadhi patta*)
~ **3 stalks**

METHOD

~ Cook the yam and banana in 1½ cups water. Add red chilli powder, turmeric powder, and salt and cook on high heat for 20 minutes.

~ Mix in the coconut paste and bring the mixture to the boil. Reduce heat and cook till the gravy thickens.

~ **For the tempering**, heat the oil in a small pan; add the mustard seeds. When they start to splutter, add dried red chilies and sauté for a few minutes till fragrant, shaking the pan occasionally. Add the remaining ingredients and fry, stirring constantly, till the coconut turns brown.

~ Pour the tempering into the curry and mix well.

~ Serve hot.

Kushamand Kautuhal

BRAHMANDA—*the metaphysical cosmic egg—has inspired countless scientific investigations and the pumpkin, resembling it in shape, in this avatar arouses culinary curiosity. Hence the name.*

INGREDIENTS

SERVES 5-6

Pumpkin (*kaddu*), cut, cored
~ 1 kg / 2.2 lb

Mustard (*sarson*) oil
~ 2 tbsp / 30 ml / 1 fl oz

Asafoetida (*hing*)
~ a small pinch

Onion seeds (*kalonji*)
~ 1 tsp / 3 gm

Cumin (*jeera*) seeds
~ 1 tsp / 2 gm

Mustard seeds (*rai*)
~ ½ tsp / 1½ gm

Fennel (*moti saunf*) seeds
~ 1 tsp / 2½ gm

Fenugreek seeds (*methi dana*)
~ ½ tsp / 2 gm

Poppy seeds (*khus khus*), ground to paste
~ 1 tsp / 3 gm

Jaggery (*gur*), grated
~ 50 gm / 1¾ oz

Lemon (*nimbu*) juice
~ 1 tbsp / 15 ml

Salt to taste

Dried red chillies (*sookhi lal mirch*), lightly fried
~ 4-6

Green chillies, chopped for garnishing

Green coriander (*hara dhaniya*), fresh, chopped for garnishing

METHOD

~ Boil the pumpkin with enough water to cover in a pan.

~ Heat the oil in a pan; add asafoetida, onion seeds, cumin seeds, mustard seeds, fennel seeds, and fenugreek seeds. When the seeds start crackling and releasing their aroma, add the poppy seed paste and stir for a minute.

~ Add the boiled pumpkin after draining the excess water. Mash to pulp, add jaggery and lemon juice. Cook for about 3 minutes to blend all the ingredients well. Remove from heat and temper with lightly fried red chillies.

~ Serve hot garnished with green chillies and green coriander, accompanied with puri or roti or steamed rice.

Dalika

LENTILS *that have been ground to split the seeds qualify for this epithet. Boiled lentils are the preferred source of easy-to-digest proteins in India and are paired invariably with rice or roti.*

INGREDIENTS

SERVES 4

Split red gram (*arhar dal*), soaked in water for 30 minutes, drained
~ **1¼ cups / 250 gm / 9 oz**

Coriander (*dhaniya*) powder
~ **1½ tsp / 4½ gm**

Turmeric (*haldi*) powder
~ **1 tsp / 3 gm**

Salt to taste

Ghee
~ **2 tbsp / 30 gm / 1 oz**

Cumin (*jeera*) seeds
~ **½ tsp / 1 gm**

Cloves (*laung*)
~ **3-4**

Dried red chillies (*sookhi lal mirch*)
~ **2-3**

Asafoetida (*hing*)
~ **a pinch**

Garlic (*lasan*), chopped
~ **2 tsp**

Ginger (*adrak*), chopped
~ **2 tsp**

Green coriander (*hara dhaniya*), fresh, chopped for garnishing

METHOD

~ Boil 4 cups of water in a pan; add the dal, coriander powder, turmeric powder, and salt. Cover and continue to boil till the water has almost evaporated and the dal is cooked. Add some boiled water, cover again and cook on low heat till it is soft to touch, but not overcooked.

~ Heat the ghee in a pan; splutter the cumin seeds, cloves, dried red chillies, and asafoetida. Add garlic and ginger; sauté till golden brown.

~ Remove and pour over the dal; mix well.

~ Serve hot garnished with green coriander and accompanied with steamed rice.

Dincharya

The Hindu soul recipes work best when they are savoured at the time prescribed for daily meals. Ancient wisdom advises us to eat only when hungry, at regular intervals and at the time set for the morning, day and night meals. We are advised to eat slowly, masticate properly, relish the food and not be distracted while eating. *Anna* (food) is considered Brahma and the taste represents Vishnu. The one who consumes food himself is the representative of Shiva. Dining thus mirrors creation, preservation and dissolution.

Batika

THE *name in original Sanskrit means a small tablet. In Hindi it is called* barhi *or the elder. This dried spicy dumpling is enjoyable on its own or used to spike another dish.*

INGREDIENTS

SERVES 4

Black gram dumplings
(*urad dal barhi*)
~ **250 gm / 9 oz**

Yoghurt (*dahi*)
~ **150 gm / 5 oz**

Coriander (*dhaniya*)
powder
~ **1 tbsp / 9 gm**

Red chilli powder
~ **1 tsp / 3 gm**

Turmeric (*haldi*) powder
~ **1 tsp / 3 gm**

Ghee
~ **5 tbsp / 75 gm / 2½ oz**

Cumin (*jeera*) seeds
~ **2 tsp / 4 gm**

Ginger (*adrak*) paste
~ **3½ tsp / 20 gm**

Garlic (*lasan*) paste
~ **1¾ tsp / 10 gm**

Salt to taste

Fenugreek (*methi*) powder
~ **a generous pinch**

Green coriander (*hara dhaniya*), chopped
~ **1 tbsp / 4 gm**

METHOD

~ Mix the yoghurt with coriander powder, red chilli powder, and turmeric powder; whisk to mix well.

~ Heat the ghee in a pan; add cumin seeds and stir on medium heat until they begin to splutter. Add ginger and garlic pastes; stir-fry for about 45 seconds. Remove the pan from the heat, stir-in the yoghurt mixture and return to heat. Cook till specks of fat begin to appear on the surface. Add 4 cups of water and salt; bring the mixture to the boil.

~ Add the black gram dumplings and continue to boil. Reduce heat and simmer, stirring regularly, till the gravy is of thin sauce-like consistency. Sprinkle fenugreek powder, stir and remove from heat. Adjust seasoning.

~ Serve hot garnished with green coriander.

Alaukika

LITERALLY *'out of this world', this sublime marrow delicacy from Kashmir transports us to an ethereal realm.*

INGREDIENTS

SERVES 5-6

Bottle gourd (*lauki*), scraped, washed, cut into 1"-thick rounds
~ 1 kg / 2.2 lb

Mustard (*sarson*) oil
~ ¼ cup / 60 ml / 2 fl oz

Asafoetida (*hing*)
~ a small pinch

Kashmiri red chilli powder, dissolved in 1 tsp water
~ 1 tbsp / 9 gm

Dried ginger powder (*sonth*)
~ 1 tsp / 3 gm

Yoghurt (*dahi*), hung
~ 200 gm / 7 oz

Fennel (*moti saunf*) powder
~ 1 tsp / 3 gm

Garam masala
~ 1 tsp / 3 gm

Salt to taste

METHOD

~ Heat the oil in a thick-bottomed pan till it starts smoking. Reduce heat, add asafoetida and mix till it dissolves.

~ Add red chilli mixture and stir briskly for 15 seconds. Add the bottle gourd and fry very lightly for about a minute and a half.

~ Add the dried ginger powder and yoghurt; stir well. Add the fennel powder, garam masala, and salt. Cook covered, stirring occasionally. Remove when done, the vegetable should retain a little bite.

~ The dish can be served draped in its sauce with a creamy consistency or the spicy slices can be enjoyed separately.

Panchamrit

This liquid concoction prepared by blending milk, honey, ghee, yoghurt and *Gangajal* is likened to *amrit*—the nectar that grants the boon of immortality to the Hindu gods. It is imbibed just before partaking *prasad* (graceful blessings) with the invocation: 'I sip the water that has emanated from the feet of Vishnu, and anoint myself with it. May it protect me from disease and untimely death!' Its lineage is traced to *madhupark*—an ambrosial refreshing intoxicant free drink dating back to Vedic times—that preceded the myriad fruit or flower-flavoured syrups in the succeeding millennia.

Kshirika

ACCORDING *to ayurveda, kshirika is a wonderfully balanced food, blending rice and lentils in an appetizing and easily digestible form. It is equally suitable for the convalescent as well as the* sadhak *(spiritual seeker).*

INGREDIENTS

SERVES 4

Rice
~ ½ cup / 100 gm / 3½ oz

Split green gram (*moong dal*)
~ ½ cup / 100 gm / 3½ oz

Ginger (*adrak*) paste
~ 1 tbsp / 18 gm

Aniseed (*saunf*) paste
~ 2 tsp / 10 gm

Salt to taste

Ghee
~ 2 tsp / 10 gm

Aniseed
~ 1 tsp / 2½ gm

Bay leaves (*tej patta*)
~ 2

METHOD

~ Boil rice and split green gram in a deep pan with enough water to cover. Add ginger paste, aniseed paste, and salt. Cook until the mixture reaches a soft thick consistency.

~ Heat the ghee to smoking in a pan; reduce heat and sauté the aniseed and bay leaves until the bay leaves turn colour. Pour over the rice and dal mixture and cover.

~ Serve hot.

Mahashali

Basmati may be the aromatic rice produced in India that is internationally renowned but in ancient Indian texts the pride of place is given to Mahashali. A disciple of Xuan Zang has written, 'Mahashali is as large as the black bean and when cooked its aroma and sheen are unmatched. It grows only in Magadha and is considered fit enough only for princes or high priests.'

Haak

ALL *leafy greens are called* shaak *in Sanskrit and the vernacular Hindi and Punjabi* saag *derives from it. Haak is the way the word is pronounced in the Vale and is reserved for the incomparably flavourful Kashmiri spinach.*

INGREDIENTS

SERVES 4

Kashmiri spinach (*haak*)
~ **1 kg / 2.2 lb**

Sugar
~ **1 tsp / 3 gm**

Mustard (*sarson*) oil
~ **1 tbsp / 15 ml**

Asafoetida (*hing*)
~ **a pinch**

Red chilli powder
~ **½ tsp / 1½ gm**

Cumin (*jeera*) powder
~ **½ tsp / 1½ gm**

Dried ginger powder
(*sonth*)
~ **1 tsp / 3 gm**

Salt to taste

Kashmiri *barhi* (large
tablet incorporating
Kashmiri dried spices),
optional
~ **1 tsp**

Fenugreek seeds (*methi
dana*)
~ **½ tsp / 2¼ gm**

METHOD

~ Boil the *haak* in 2 cups of water in the pan. Reduce heat and simmer for 20 minutes. When it softens, add sugar and remove from heat after a few minutes. Retain some gravy.

~ Heat the mustard oil in a pan; add asafoetida, red chilli powder, cumin powder, dried ginger powder, salt, Kashmiri *barhi* (optional), and fenugreek seeds; fry for a few seconds. Add the boiled greens to this and stir well.

Shaak

THE *goddess of plants is called Shakambhaare but the word* shaak *describes only a small part of her vast domain. The term generically covers all leafy greens, specifically it means spinach or mustard. It is considered pure food* (satvik).

INGREDIENTS

SERVES 4

Mustard (*sarson*) leaves, roughly chopped
~ 750 gm / 27 oz

Spinach (*palak*), roughly chopped
~ 250 gm / 9 oz

White radish (*mooli*) leaves, roughly chopped
~ 100 gm / 3½ oz

Bathua, roughly chopped
~ 30 gm / 1 oz

Green chillies, slit, deseeded
~ 8

Ginger (*adrak*), diced
~ 4 tbsp / 30 gm

Mustard (*sarson*) oil
~ ¼ cup / 60 ml / 2 fl oz

Rice
~ 45 gm / 1½ oz

Salt to taste

Maize flour (*bajra*)
~ 1½ tbsp / 15 gm

White butter
~ 1 cup / 200 gm / 7 oz

METHOD

~ Prepare a mixture of all the ingredients except maize flour and white butter in a pan and add 8 cups of water. Bring to the boil; reduce heat to low and simmer for about 1 hour 45 minutes or until the greens are tender. Remove the pan from the heat and churn with a wooden churner.

~ Return the pan to the heat and add maize flour. Cover and simmer on very low heat. Keep stirring regularly for about 1 hour. Remove and adjust the seasoning.

~ Serve hot garnished with large dollops of white butter.

Shaakaahaara

In Sanskrit the generic term for all leafy greens is *shaak* and prefixed to *ahara* (food) describes vegetarian repast. Spinach, mustard and amaranth have for thousands of years been a staple part of the Hindu diet. There are millions of Indians, usually non-vegetarians, who regularly observe a meatless day in the week or confine their diet only to vegetables for a week, fortnight or a month.

Dadimashtaka

THE *culinary octave—number eight indicated by the word* ashtaka*—led by pomegranate seeds plays a piquant symphony of tastes when paired with chick peas.*

INGREDIENTS

SERVES 4

Chick peas (*kabuli chana*), soaked in water for about 2 hours
~ 2²/₃ cups / 400 gm / 14 oz

For the muslin pouch (*potli*):
Black cardamom (*badi elaichi*)
~ 6

Cinnamon (*dalchini*), 1" sticks
~ 4

Cloves (*laung*)
~ 4

Ginger (*adrak*), crushed
~ 1"

Tea leaves
~ 2 tsp

For the tempering:
Vegetable oil
~ 5 tbsp / 75 ml / 2½ fl oz

Cumin (*jeera*) seeds
~ 1 tsp / 3 gm

Gram flour (*besan*)
~ 1 tbsp / 10 gm

Carom (*ajwain*) seeds
~ 1 tsp / 2½ gm

Pomegranate (*anar*) powder
~ 5 tsp / 15 gm

Mango powder (*amchur*)
~ 2 tsp / 6 gm

Red chilli powder
~ 1 tsp / 3 gm

Black rock salt
~ 1 tsp / 3 gm

Fenugreek leaf (*kasoori methi*) powder, dried
~ 2 tsp / 3 gm

Salt to taste

For the garnishing:
Tomatoes, medium-sized, cut into wedges
~ 2

Onion, medium-sized, cut into rings
~ 1

Green chillies, slit, deseeded
~ 2

Lemons (*nimbu*), cut into wedges
~ 3

Ginger, juliennes, soaked in 2 tbsp lemon juice
~ 1½ tbsp / 10 gm

There is an elaborate description of the vessels in which food is served and consumed and the material used is believed to impact what is being cooked. Gold, the noble metal, is considered best; silver, bronze, brass and iron are listed in descending order. Using stoneware and clay on a regular basis is to be avoided by all those who can afford better. Wood and leafs are prescribed for ritual meals.

METHOD

~ Boil the soaked chick peas. Remove and reserve in same water for about 1 hour. Drain the water just before cooking.

~ **For the muslin pouch**, put all the ingredients mentioned in a clean muslin cloth and secure with string to make a pouch.

~ Transfer the chick peas in a pan and add 4 cups of fresh water. Bring to the boil. Reduce heat to low and remove any scum. Add 5 tsp oil and the muslin pouch; cover and simmer till cooked but firm. Just make sure that the chick peas don't get mashed and their skin remains intact. Remove and put aside.

~ **For the tempering**, heat the remaining oil in a pan; add cumin seeds. Stir on medium heat until the seeds begin to crackle. Add gram flour and stir-fry until it emits an aroma. Add the remaining ingredients and stir-fry for about a minute. Add cooked chick peas and stir till well mixed. Remove and adjust seasoning.

~ Serve hot garnished with tomatoes, onion rings, green chillies, lemon wedges, and ginger juliennes.

Thayir Sadam

THIS *is traditionally the last course in southern dining. Milky 'white as moon' yoghurt is coupled with plain steamed rice flavoured with ginger, green chillies and rendered more interesting by a tempering of curry leaves and mustard.*

INGREDIENTS

SERVES 4

Rice, soaked for 10 minutes
~ **1 cup / 200 gm / 7 oz**

Salt to taste

Yoghurt (*dahi*), whisked
~ **1¹⁄₃ cups / 350 gm / 12 oz**

Coconut (*nariyal*), grated
~ **½ cup / 60 gm / 2 oz**

Green coriander (*hara dhaniya*), chopped
~ **5 tbsp / 20 gm**

Vegetable oil
~ **2½ tbsp / 36 ml / 1¼ fl oz**

Mustard seeds (*rai*)
~ **1½ tsp / 5 gm**

Curry leaves (*kadhi patta*)
~ **a large sprig**

Bengal gram (*chana dal*)
~ **1 tsp**

Green chillies, deseeded, chopped
~ **2 tbsp / 12 gm**

Milk
~ **100 ml / 3½ fl oz**

METHOD

~ Drain the rice and replenish with fresh water. Add salt and boil until slightly overcooked. Drain. Cool.

~ In a bowl, mix the yoghurt, rice, coconut, and green coriander together.

~ Heat the oil in a pan; add mustard seeds, curry leaves, Bengal gram, and green chillies; sauté on medium heat for 30 seconds. Pour this tempering over the rice and yoghurt mixture and cool.

~ Add milk, stir and refrigerate.

Dhanya

DURING *Pongal* (*the harvest festival in South India*) *the pot of milk on the fire is happily allowed to boil over to symbolize overflowing joy. It seems appropriate to rename this traditional Pongal recipe indicating gratitude and bliss* (dhanya).

METHOD

~ Boil green gram in water, drain and mash.

~ Dry roast rice *rawa* and add to the green gram with salt and 4 cups water. Cook together on low heat till well cooked and grainy with water fully absorbed.

~ Heat the oil or ghee in a frying pan; add all the seasoning ingredients, cashew nuts and black pepper powder; sauté together. Remove from heat and add to the rice mixture.

INGREDIENTS

SERVES 6

Green gram (*moong dal*), dry roasted
~ **1 cup / 200 gm / 7 oz**

Water
~ **2 cups / 500 ml / 16 fl oz**

Rice *rawa* (coarsely ground rice resembling semolina)
~ **2 cups / 400 gm / 14 oz**

Salt to taste

Vegetable oil / Ghee
~ **¾ cup / 180 ml / 6 fl oz**

Cashew nuts (*kaju*)
~ **12**

Black pepper (*kali mirch*) powder
~ **1 tsp / 3 gm**

For the seasoning:
Mustard seeds (*rai*)
~ **1 tsp / 3 gm**

Dried red chillies (*sookhi lal mirch*)
~ **3**

Curry leaves (*kadhi patta*)
~ **6**

Asafoetida (*hing*)
~ **a pinch**

Juice of lemon (*nimbu*), optional
~ **1**

Mahakoshtika

THE *'grand gourd'—as its name leaves us in no doubt—brooks no rivals in the realm of squashes. It is reckoned among the purest of vegetables that has for centuries been cherished as a fast cooking, easily digestible and tasty ingredient.*

INGREDIENTS

SERVES 2-4

Wax gourd (*torai*),
washed, scraped, cut into
thin rounds
~ 1 kg / 2.2 lb

Ghee
~ 1 tbsp / 15 gm

Cumin (*jeera*) seeds
~ 1 tsp / 2 gm

Green chillies, wiped
cleaned, slit lengthwise
~ 2-3

Salt to taste

METHOD

~ Heat the ghee in a thick-bottomed pan; add the cumin seeds. When the seeds begin to crackle, add the wax gourd and green chillies. Sprinkle salt, reduce heat and cook covered till all the moisture evaporates. Do not add any water.

~ Remove and serve hot.

Lavana

Charak, the pioneering scholar, who compiled a compendium on ayurveda lists five types of salt—*saindhava* (rock salt obtained from the province of Sindha), *samudra* (produced by evaporating saline sea water), *vida* (black rock salt), *pansuja* (earth salt) and *audvida* (efflorescent salt). Shushruth, another scholar of ayurveda, lists nine more mineral salts derived from both sodium and potassium.

Accompaniments

When the appetite is sluggish, for whatever reason, the digestive fire needs to be stoked and this is exactly what an *uddipaka* (aperitif) does—it literally acts as a catalyst. There is a great variety of pickles prepared seasonally in different regions of the subcontinent that masterfully blend the *katu* (bitter), *amla* (sour), *tikshna* (pungent), *kashaya* (astringent), *lavana* (salty), and *madhur* (sweet) *rasa* with traces of other therapeutic ingredients in a very appetizing manner.

Rasam

THIS *is literally the essence—nutritious extract of lentils flavoured with tamarind or tomatoes then tempered, comprising the first course in traditional South Indian meal. An aromatic aperitif that comes closest to a soup.*

INGREDIENTS

SERVES 4

Lentil (*masoor dal*), soaked for 1 hour, drained
~ 30 gm / 1 oz

Split red gram (*arhar dal*), soaked for 1 hour, drained
~ 30 gm / 1 oz

Tomatoes, washed, chopped
~ 350 gm / 12 oz

Capsicum (*Shimla mirch*), deseeded, diced
~ 30 gm / 1 oz

Green coriander (*hara dhaniya*), chopped
~ 30 gm / 1 oz

Mint (*pudina*) leaves, chopped
~ 30 gm / 1 oz

Curry leaves (*kadhi patta*), washed
~ a large sprig

Black peppercorns (*sabut kali mirch*), crushed
~ 1 tsp / 4 gm

Tamarind (*imli*) pulp
~ 60 gm / 2 oz

Rasam powder
~ 1½ tsp / 5 gm

Jaggery (*gur*)
~ 15 gm

Lemons (*nimbu*), cut into wedges
~ 2

Salt to taste

For the tempering:
Vegetable oil
~ 1 tbsp / 15 ml

Mustard seeds (*rai*)
~ 1 tsp / 3 gm

Green coriander, chopped
~ ¼ cup / 15 gm

Curry leaves, washed
~ 10

Green chillies, slit, deseeded, chopped
~ 3-4

Asafoetida (*hing*)
~ a pinch

METHOD

~ Put the drained dals in a pot; add approximately 6 cups of fresh water, tomatoes, capsicum, green coriander, mint leaves, curry leaves, and black pepper powder; bring to the boil and then simmer for 45 minutes. Strain, add tamarind pulp, *rasam* powder, and jaggery; bring to the boil again and remove.

~ **For the tempering**, heat the oil in a pan; add all the ingredients and sauté on medium heat for a few seconds. Pour in the soup and bring to the boil. Adjust the seasoning.

~ Warm 4 cups in a hot case, pour equal quantities of the soup in each and serve with lemon wedges on the side.

Susheetalam

THIS *'cold drink'* does not only quench thirst but cools down the whole body. For generations, Indians prepare this festive drink, also called thandai, *for Holi—the festival of colours in spring.* Susheetalam *or the supreme cooler is an apt name.*

METHOD

~ Grind the almonds and pistachios to a thick paste along with all the other spices. Add cold water to the ground paste and mix well. Strain through a damp muslin cloth.

~ Add the milk and sugar; mix well.

~ Serve chilled garnished with rose petals.

INGREDIENTS

SERVES 4

Cold milk
~ 2½ cups / 600 ml / 19 fl oz

Almonds (*badam*), soaked in water, peeled
~ 8

Pistachios (*pista*), soaked in water, peeled
~ 8

Poppy seeds (*khus khus*)
~ 1 tsp / 3 gm

Black peppercorns (*sabut kali mirch*)
~ 4

Cinnamon (*dalchini*) powder
~ ½ tsp

Aniseed (*saunf*)
~ 1 tsp / 2½ gm

Melon (*magaz*) seeds
~ 12

Nutmeg (*jaiphal*) powder
~ a pinch

Water to grind
~ ½ cup / 120 ml / 4 fl oz

Cold water
~ 2 cups / 500 ml / 16 fl oz

Sugar
~ 6 tsp / 18 gm

Fresh pink rose petals for garnishing
~ a few

Raita

SPICED *up yoghurt paired with chopped vegetables and at times with fruits, appears as an accompaniment on most Indian menus. The one served in Uttaranchal is pungent in a* satvik *manner.*

INGREDIENTS

SERVES 4-5

Cucumbers (*khira*),
medium-sized, peeled,
cored, grated
~ **4 (1 kg / 2.2 lb)**

Yoghurt (*dahi*)
~ **400 gm / 14 oz**

Mustard seeds (*rai*),
ground to a fine paste
~ **2 tsp / 6 gm**

Salt to taste

Turmeric (*haldi*) powder,
optional
~ **a small pinch**

Green chillies, chopped
~ **6**

Green coriander (*hara dhaniya*), fresh, coarsely chopped
~ **½ cup / 25 gm**

METHOD

~ Squeeze the grated cucumber to drain the excess water.

~ Beat the yoghurt lightly and blend well with mustard paste, salt, and turmeric powder. Add the cucumber and mix well.

~ Let the mixture rest for 3-4 hours or overnight in the fridge before using. (The quantity of mustard paste may be adjusted according to individual tolerance.)

~ Serve garnished with green chillies and green coriander.

Haldi

Haridra or *haldi* or turmeric is a rhizome believed to be native to India. It has always been accorded a pride of place in rituals. Considered particularly auspicious, it is used to colour the palms of a bride and to dye clothes to be worn on joyous occasions like marriages. *Haldi* is excluded from the diet during the period of mourning. Modern researches have proved that many of the claims about turmeric's medicinal properties are indeed true.

Thalipeeth

OCCUPYING *the pride of place, as its name indicates, on* thali *(the traditional Indian dining plate) is this multi-grain bread that is quintessential basic food—unadorned nourishment for body and soul.*

INGREDIENTS

SERVES 12

Thalipeeth flour (see below) ~ **1 cup**

Green chillies, chopped ~ **1 tbsp / 6 gm**

Ginger (*adrak*), chopped ~ **1 tbsp / 7½ gm**

Onion, finely chopped ~ **1**

Red chilli powder ~ **1 tsp / 3 gm**

Yoghurt (*dahi*), sour ~ **½ cup / 125 gm / 4 oz**

Tomato, finely chopped ~ **1**

Sesame seeds (*til*), roasted ~ **1 tbsp / 10 gm**

Clove-cardamom (*laung-elaichi*) powder ~ **½ tsp / 1½ gm**

Coriander-cumin (*dhaniya-jeera*) powder ~ **½ tsp / 1½ gm**

Black pepper (*kali mirch*) powder ~ **¼ tsp**

Salt to taste

Vegetable oil for frying
For the *thalipeeth* flour: Mix together
Rice ~ **1 cup / 200 gm / 7 oz**

Wholewheat flour (*atta*) ~ **¼ cup / 37 gm / 1¼ oz**

Dark millet (*bajra*) ~ **¼ cup**

White millet (*jowar*) ~ **¼ cup**

Bengal gram (*chana dal*) ~ **¼ cup / 50 gm / 1¾ oz**

Coriander (*dhaniya*) seeds ~ **½ tsp / 1 gm**

Cumin (*jeera*) seeds ~ **½ tsp / 1 gm**

Black peppercorns (*sabut kali mirch*) ~ **½ tsp / 2 gm**

Fenugreek seeds (*methi dana*) ~ **½ tsp / 2¼ gm**

Clove (*laung*) powder ~ **½ tsp / 1½ gm**

Black cardamom (*badi elaichi*) powder ~ **½ tsp / 1½ gm**

METHOD

~ Sift the flour on to a tray, add all the ingredients except oil. Make a bay in the middle, pour a little water and knead to obtain soft dough. Divide the dough equally into small balls. Roll each ball out on a rolling board and press lightly with your palm to make small discs of approximately 3" in diameter.

~ Heat a *tawa* (griddle) with 1 tbsp oil; place a disc flat over it. Apply a little oil on the top surface, cover the pan and cook on low heat. Turn it over and cook the other side.

~ When it turns light brown, remove from heat. Repeat with the other balls.

Haritima

REFRESHINGLY *emerald hued, this chutney blends three greens—coriander, mint and green chillies. It may be prepared thick like a draping sauce or of pouring consistency.*

INGREDIENTS

SERVES 5-6

Green coriander (*hara dhaniya*), chopped
~ **1 cup / 50 gm / 1¾ oz**

Mint (*pudina*) leaves, chopped
~ **½ cup / 20 gm**

Green chillies
~ **4**

Ginger (*adrak*), chopped
~ **½ tbsp / 4 gm**

Garlic (*lasan*), chopped
~ **1 tbsp / 6 gm**

Lemon (*nimbu*) juice
~ **2 tbsp / 30 ml / 1 fl oz**

Black salt (*kala namak*)
~ **a pinch**

Salt to taste

METHOD

~ Put all the ingredients together in a blender and make a semi-liquid paste by adding chilled water.

~ Serve as required.

Digestive Fire

When the metabolism is sluggish digestion is impaired and it is said that the digestive fire is burning slow. This condition is known as *mandagni*. If the flames are not stoked with appetizers and aperitifs weakness may result. On the contrary if the rate of metabolism is abnormally high the body is denied adequate nourishment. This condition is called *jatharagni*. For proper nourishment of the body and the soul a proper balance has to be maintained.

Shveta

THE *name* Shveta *translates as white and it symbolizes unblemished virtue and purity. This fair-complexioned chutney combining two types of white—the radish and the yoghurt—is exceptionally mild and stands out due to its exceptional hue.*

METHOD

~ Sprinkle a little salt on the radish and keep aside for about 15 minutes to drain off excess water.

~ Add all the ingredients; mix well.

~ Serve chilled.

INGREDIENTS

SERVES 5-6

Radish (*mooli*), grated
~ **80 gm / 2¾ oz**

Lemon (*nimbu*) juice
~ **2 tsp / 10 ml**

Green chilli paste
~ **1 tbsp / 15 gm**

Black salt (*kala namak*)
~ **a pinch**

Yoghurt (*dahi*), whisked
~ **45 gm / 1½ oz**

Salt to tast**e**

Sharkara

Historically India has evoked visions of a land where rivers of milk and honey flow. The Greek traveller, Megasthenes, who visited India in the wake of Alexander's invasion was amazed to see Indian's drink honey out of giant bamboo canes. He may have been confused by the Sanskrit synonym for sugarcane—*madhutrina* or honey-bearing grass. However, no one can dispute that the Indians were the first to taste sugar and share it with the rest of the world.

Amlan

THE amla *berry is the quintessential reservoir of the astringent taste; rich in vitamins. It is believed to gift unalloyed joy to whoever partakes it. And this is exactly what* amlan *indicates.*

INGREDIENTS

MAKES 1 KG (APPROX.)

Indian gooseberries (*amla*),
washed
~ 1 kg / 2.2 lb

Lemon (*nimbu*)
~ 1

Sugar
~ 1.5 kg / 3.3 lb

METHOD

~ Pat dry the Indian gooseberries and prick well. Soak in water overnight.

~ Boil sugar dissolved in about 4½ cups of water to obtain a syrup of two string consistency.

~ Squeeze lemon juice and remove the scum that rises to the surface.

~ Add the pricked Indian gooseberries and boil for 3-5 minutes in the syrup. Remove and cool.

~ Pack in clean, dry airtight containers. Let it mature for a couple of days.

Triphala

The sublime trinity of *harad*, *baheda* and *amla* recalls to mind the *trimourti* symbolizing Brahma, Vishnu and Mahesh—gods in the Hindu pantheon that symbolize creation, preservation and destruction—to dispose of waste and prepare the ground for regeneration. The three ingredients blended together are termed *triphala*—literally, three fruits—that are believed to have miraculous therapeutic properties.

Kalyanankar

BAEL, *a fruit believed to be a beloved of the ascetic Lord Shiva, has many beneficial properties according to ayurveda. Its preserve served as a dessert helps digestion and builds immunity against debilitating ailments—truly a benefactor* (kalyanankar).

INGREDIENTS

SERVES 4-5

Bael, medium-sized **~ 2-3**	Sugar **~ 1 kg / 2.2 lb**

METHOD

~ Cut open the fruit in half and remove the kernel carefully. Slice to obtain 4 pieces to a half. Remove the fibrous tissue with a sharp knife.

~ Boil the sugar dissolved in about a litre of water to obtain a syrup of two string consistency.

~ Boil the sliced bael in this syrup for about 5 minutes. Remove from heat, cool and store in dry jars.

Phalahar

A diet exclusively of fruits is considered the most *satvik* repast—ideal for those who wish to progress speedily along the spiritual path. Fruits have formed a part of our diet from the cave-dwelling hunting gathering days when our ancestors had not yet learned the art of growing food. The hermits and the sages who had renounced the world sustained themselves primarily on roots and fruits (*kanda mool phal*).

Desserts

For Hindus the essence of life is sweetness. The Lord himself is sweetness incarnate and anything touched by His grace becomes sweet. Can one aspire for anything other than sweetness? Sweet beginnings are a part of this land's glorious traditions. Every ritual invocation of the deities begins with the offering of *mishthann* (sweet foods).

Indian epics are replete with reverential references to sweets. For example, Lakshmi and Vishnu dwell in the *Ksheer Sagar* (a celestial Ocean of Milk) that has given its name to the ubiquitous *kheer*—the popular north Indian concoction of rice and sweetened milk. In many other parts of our vast and varied land it is known as *payas* or *payasam*. (The word *payas* also means milk.) Vinayak Ganesh, the Hindu god of auspicious beginnings, is inseparable from the *modak* or *laddoo* prepared with a variety of grains. The supreme flute-player, dark-skinned Sri Krishna is depicted as an adorable addict to *makhan-misri* (freshly churned butter rendered even more tempting with crystal sugar).

Apooravapoopa

THIS *marvellous confection (apooravapoopa) is a nutritious sweet dating back to the Vedic period claiming a most ancient lineage. It has evolved across millennia, and is encountered in many forms ranging from an unadorned dumpling to a dazzling pancake.*

INGREDIENTS

SERVES 6-8

Yoghurt (*dahi*),
unsweetened
~ 1 cup / 250 gm / 9 oz

Refined flour (*maida*)
~ 2 tbsp / 20 gm

Aniseed (*saunf*)
~ 1 tsp / 2½ gm

Ghee
~ 100 gm / 3½ oz

For the syrup:
Sugar
~ 1 cup / 225 gm / 8 oz

Water
~ 2 cups / 500 ml / 16 fl oz

METHOD

~ Blend the yoghurt with the flour in a bowl. Add aniseed and mix well.

~ Heat the ghee in a pan; add I tbsp of yoghurt at a time and fry until brown and crisp at the edges. Remove and drain the excess oil on absorbent kitchen towels. Repeat till all the batter is used up.

~ **For the syrup,** mix the sugar in cold water and stir until the sugar dissolves. Cook the sugar mixture on medium heat and bring to the boil. Boil until the syrup is thick. Remove and keep aside to cool.

~ Place the pancakes in the syrup, one at a time, as they are fried.

Ghrit

According to ayurveda, the best cooking medium is *ghrit* or ghee in common parlance obtained from cow's milk. The best quality cow ghee is a pale golden liquid. Buffalo ghee is off-white in colour and has much greater fat content. Ghee was described by the Buddha as quintessential *satvik* food 'full of soul qualities'. Aged ghee matured between ten to hundred years is called *kumbhaghrit* and that of even older vintage is *mahaghrit*. Mature ghee is believed to be an exceptional tonic with rejuvenating qualities.

Shrikhanda

A *'slice of riches'* is what shrikhanda *aptly communicates to all those it gives unalloyed joy. Satin smooth hung yoghurt flavoured subtly with cardamom with just a hint of sweet and redolent with saffron is truly sublime.*

INGREDIENTS

SERVES 6

Yoghurt (*dahi*), hung in a muslin to drain whey overnight
~ 1 kg / 2.2 lb

Castor sugar
~ ½ cup / 100 gm / 3½ oz

Saffron (*kesar*), soaked in 1 tbsp milk
~ 1 tsp

Green cardamom (*choti elaichi*) seeds, crushed
~ 1 tsp / 3 gm

Pistachios (*pista*), blanched, slivered
~ 8-10

METHOD

~ Put the yoghurt cheese in a bowl. Add sugar, gradually, whisking until fluffy.

~ Pour the saffron mixture, and sprinkle green cardamom; whisk again and cool before serving.

Madhuram

When humankind was food gathering—in the pre-hunting food gathering stage—the survival of the species depended on distinguishing between nutritious and poisonous substances. A fruit or berry just right for consumption overflowed with sweetness, a sour or bitter bite indicated danger. Sweet, in course of time, became synonymous with goodness—sweet smell, sweet voice and sweet temper.

Payasam

PAYASAM *or* kheer *is often referred to as* parmanna *(the ultimate food). According to the Hindu myth, Lord Vishnu reclining in repose on his 'bed' —celestial serpent Sheshnag—floats eternally on an ocean of* ksheer *or* kheer.

INGREDIENTS

SERVES 4

Milk
~ 8 cups / 2 lt / 64 fl oz

Rice
~ 1 tbsp

Vermicelli (*sevain*)
~ 20 gm

Coconut (*nariyal*), freshly grated
~ 2 tbsp

Almonds (*badam*)
~ 15-20

Pistachios (*pista*)
~ 10

Raisins (*kishmish*), soaked in rose water
~ 2 tbsp

Green cardamom (*choti elaichi*) seeds, crushed
~ 3

Sugar
~ 10 tbsp / 150 gm / 5 oz

METHOD

~ Soak the rice in ½ cup water for 30 minutes. Drain.

~ Dry roast the vermicelli without letting it turn dark brown.

~ Boil the milk in a thick-bottomed pan. Reduce heat and simmer, stirring constantly, until reduced to one-third.

~ Add the rice and continue to boil on low medium heat for 10 minutes. Add vermicelli and boil for another 5 minutes. Add coconut and boil for 5 minutes more.

~ Remove from heat stir in the sugar and dried fruits. Sprinkle the crushed cardamom seeds and serve hot or cold as it is equally flavourful.

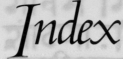

Index